Finding Home

by Diane Jerome
Illustrated by Pat Paris

Glenview, Illinois • Boston, Massachusetts • Chandler, Arizona
Upper Saddle River, New Jersey

The Chumash Girl

Long ago, the Chumash Indians lived near the ocean. Shells from the ocean were important to them. They made things from the shells.

Anacapa was a Chumash girl. One day, Anacapa wanted to collect shells. She walked to the ocean.

footprints

It was a sunny day. Anacapa saw footprints on the trail. She heard a whisper. It was only the wind.

Then she heard a noise in the bushes. What could it be? Anacapa hurried to the beach.

Anacapa at the Beach

At the beach, Anacapa saw many shells. Some were pink. Others were white. They were all pretty.

Anacapa kept walking. She was very busy collecting shells. She did not see that it was getting dark.

Night at the Beach

Time passed. The sun set. It got very dark. It was too dark to get home. Anacapa needed a place to sleep. She found a safe cave.

To feel better, she made up a song:

The sunrise on the ocean
Will soon light up the sky.
The waves out on the ocean,
They sing a lullaby.

Looking for Anacapa

Anacapa's parents were worried. No one knew where she was. Everyone looked for her. They looked all night. No one found Anacapa.

Morning

At last, the sun rose. Anacapa woke up. She needed to eat. She ate berries and clams.

Anacapa knew she should get home. Her mother and father must be worried. Maybe they were mad too!

Going Home!

Anacapa looked up. She saw a condor. The big bird could lead her home!

Anacapa ran to the trail. Her mother was there! She shouted with joy! They hugged each other. No one was mad. Everyone was happy. Anacapa was home again!

Morning

At last, the sun rose. Anacapa woke up. She needed to eat. She ate berries and clams.

Anacapa knew she should get home. Her mother and father must be worried. Maybe they were mad too!

Going Home!

Anacapa looked up. She saw a condor. The big bird could lead her home!

Anacapa ran to the trail. Her mother was there! She shouted with joy! They hugged each other. No one was mad. Everyone was happy. Anacapa was home again!